Emily Bock
The Torture of Your Love

© 2021 Emily Bock.

Emily Bock
The Torture of Your Love
Publisher's Note: This is a work of fiction. Names, characters, places, and incidents are a product of the author's imagination. Locales and public names are sometimes used for atmospheric purposes. Any resemblance to actual people, living or dead, or to businesses, companies, events, institutions, or locales is completely coincidental.

All rights reserved. No part of this publication may be reproduced, stored in a retrieval system or transmitted in any form or by any means, electronic, mechanical, photocopying, recording or otherwise without the prior permission of the publisher or in accordance with the provisions of the Copyright, Designs and Patents Act 1988 or under the terms of any licence permitting limited copying issued by the Copyright Licensing Agency.

Published by:
Madhouse Media Publishing
www.madhousemedia.com.au

ISBN: 978-0-9925713-6-8

Written and Distributed by:
Emily Bock
www.hippiethinking.com

Illustrated by:
Brad Collins

Printed edition IngramSpark 2022

Chapters

Falling Into Forbidden Arms 9

Butterflies of heaven	10
Your anxiety gives me anxiety	11
Golden children	12
A lake in Africa	13
Fractures in my universe	15
Please, catch me at the end of my chaîné turn	16
Wrong person	18
Reminded of you	19

Remind Me I'm Inadequate 21

Mould me pretty	23
Junkyard of rotted flesh	24
Under the moon's flame	25
Losing me	26
No love in Antartica	27
The ringing in my ears	28
Oatmeal	29
Battlefield of love	30

Body Aches 33

Train of thought	34
A sad skeleton	36
Cascade	37
Behind my bedroom door	39
Not dead yet	40
Fractures in my chest	41
Over filled mugs & over filled regrets	42
Binge eating	43
Forest green eyes stirred by mother earth	44
Let me slip, I'm not ready to get over it	45

The Torture *of* Your Love

—— a collection of poems by ——
Emily Bock

Falling Into Forbidden Arms

one

Butterflies of heaven

Let us waltz across the stepping stones
Taking us up to the sky.
Disco ball sun gambols on the Summer horizon,
Mango air infiltrates our lungs.
Love permeates my knitted sweater
It drips like sweat down my centre line
Tickles my stomach
> *Butterflies.*

Whistling words we sung
Our feet flow as one
Climbing stairs until the moon's cycle is undone
Twirling until
> Tomorrow
>> never
>>> comes.

Your anxiety gives me anxiety

Your kiss presses unspirited
against my cherry lip balm.
Verbalise the menacing, jagged thoughts
slicing the lobe of your brain.
You stay quiet.
Warm tears secrete from your sorry eyes
droplets shaped as letters,
I could assimilate what you won't say.
The tears magnetise to the pit of your palms
where your head hides,
Is it hurting yet?
    Anxiety;
     a mental condition that loves throwing knives,
deep scars slice,
and carve a false being.
You lock feelings behind bars
and lose the key
My heart is squirming impatiently
tugging, pretending I'm a locksmith.
I want to preserve what's left
of your rust gnawed ankles,
unanchor your floundering soul,
Reach for your hand,
convince you

                  I give a damn.

Golden children

> Golden auras
>   glitter your figure
>
> passion to feel love
>   litter our fingers.

A lake in Africa

Hazy gleaming sun,
I'm leaning over the border,
A silhouette of me
Lay on the water.
Pounding chest
Like African drums
Welcome our lost spirits
Roaming the currents.
I meet you at last,
Fall into still waves
Ripples roll the movie film
Our spirits float away.

Fractures in my universe

My crystallic heart,
constellations glimmered its surface.
Each star was the fracture of a woeful memory,
when the hammer of the world smashed me
the fallen shards were cupped by your galaxy.

> It was suicide
> > until you *seized* me,
>
> I hadn't a purpose,
> > until you *kissed* me.

Please, catch me
at the end of my chaîné turn

We enact love on a stage,
the curtain stays closed.
Each scene ends in my apology
for hauling you over the hardships of my life
protruding like crooked nails,
by the clutch of my confidence.
It refashions your skin with gashes and whiplash
under love's command.
Life is a mockery of neglect and regret
      with that same love
           in the grip of the player's shaky hand.
My shame performs harsh adagio
yet you kiss me gracefully, forceful
enough to steady my sporadic feet.
Ballet behind a paper screen of doubt,
Why stay through the aches and pains?

Cou-de-pied on the final chord
our feet entwine
my pointe shoe like trip-wire,
into your arms
my limber body drapes.
Our tutus strip
and you tell me of the solace in my chaos,

   'To curtsy in pride with the red curtains wide,
        we can display your love & your chaos just once,
alright?'

        'Maybe in the next life,"

                      I reply.

Wrong person

The stone path we stroll,
The end is near.
Hands rip out in front of me,
Don't leave.
Clenching your coat collar,
We kiss.
My heart cripples
Like spring blossoms shrivelling.

Reminded of you

These trousers you wore
droop over my open drawers.
Scent of lavender essence
filtrates the air in between
my bedroom walls.
Your favourite pair, blotched
with spaghetti,
an unforgettable night;
engrossed by dusky skies,
enthusiastic school kids jesting in the kitchen.
I recall piles of pasta marinara
spattering the halls,
slobbered on by the memory of me sobbing
alone, dustpan and broom in hand.
You left early, and never returned.
I apologise for your filthy jeans,
Fresh air is stifling
I need perspiration and lavender embellishing
this atmosphere I live in.
They'll be on my drawers
beside the funeral flowers.

Remind Me I'm Inadequate

two

Mould me pretty

My face
was a clay model
of beauty
you mushed
between your mammoth fingers,
my identity sunken
beneath what you called
        playdough.
The lid of insecurity
slammed
over my bowed head.
I spent my days dullen
doused in oily tears.
Lather me
in gasoline
and light a fire.
If I ever feel alright
I will ignite like a sparkler.
For now,
I breathe your musty petrol
alone in my toy box
keeping packed away
awaiting your flame.

Junkyard of rotted flesh

Inadequate young me,
Petite limbs intact,
Dismantled naked heart,
Exploited and blitzed.
My withered, fetid soul
Bottled feelings since we met,
Strewed organ remains
Swept into a mount.

Under the moon's flame

Your moonlight like a white fire
Crisping my piglet skin.
Your grin is menacing
I begin crackling
Tasting of pork in twine.
Your deceit is shining
On this full moon night,
I'm burning alive,
Roasting in love
Revolving,

dying.

Losing me

I scrutinise your eyes,

>Will losing me upset you?

I scoop in my last sour mouthful
munching marrow and muscle,
my decayed molecules mush
like mouldy apple pie in saliva.
A final exhausted exhale
your name tumbling down my cheeks,
my everlasting pigment of perception is you
>*forever.*

The spoon tinks the tiling of my old room,
I perish with contentment.

>Does losing me upset you?

No love in Antarctica

Acres of ocean in front of me,
Sparsity bombards me with sanity,
My mind drifts astray
Skiing the deadly currents of waves.
Luring me in
I creep closer,
I step into insanity
And leap for my fantasy.

I paddle with indecision
In insufferable arctic water.

Accelerate after you or drown cowardly?

Salty ice blankets my skin,
I feel warmth pervading
but I'm just imagining.
Your hand melted off mine
when loving me became arduous.

I drown cowardly.

The ringing in my ears

Croaking voice
Mispitching the melody of symphonies,
Sounds ring in my memories.

I grasp for one last glance,
You continue drifting alongside the reverberations,
Demoralising tunes of miscommunication.

Oatmeal

Sweeten my melody,
sluggardly it
        sinks
        through
        dense

        h
         o
          n
           e
            y.

Bland spoonfuls
soft dripping oats
it smothers my song.
Thick milk insulates
like the walls of an isolation cell.
Sugarcoat the silenced sobbing,
I can't get through to you.
Honey oozes from my eyes,
I mangle stringiness
like a tissue in a cobweb.
I plump on the cold concrete
defeated.
I gulp…
My song of feelings for you,

        muted.

Battlefield of love

I hand my life to battlefields
victory or loss it's a poker deal.
I tap dance over the minefield,

Slash my silky circumference with your sabering flesh,
return to me, disarm our field,
You're a chemical formula I over calculated,

Clicking pens, dots and lines,
crossing T's and I's
scribbling out my identity
searching where our parallel hearts
crossed lines.

On our battlefield of love
my feet keep stirring the ground into mud
I lose limbs and other parts of me

Nimbly toe tapping forbidden feelings,
explosions erratic to rid me,
but there's a glimpse of your flame
igniting each mine I fight.

I still love you

I sacrifice all of me just for another night
hallucinating and fighting,
on our battlefield of love.

Body Aches
three

Train of thought

I did it!
I breached solitude.
I look out to the desolate landscapes
and meander an abandoned lot
deciphering where to belong.
I wander over uncanny train tracks
searching for lost goods;
    A search for you.

Night vision is blinding,
I notice a glistening surface
broad shoulders twinkle
under the luminescent moon.
Contrasted eyes stare,
I feel transparent
by a familiar, obscure silhouette.
My anxiety rampages
I'm unsure.
    It's *you*,
      I *feel* it's you.

It mixes my feelings
like a marble swirl sponge slab.
I submerge
under my buttercream blood
cheeks dyeing red,
your bittersweet presence
I'm dreading it.
Quivering and nervous giggling
you're an enticing addiction,
cravings creak my bakery floorboards
a horn blares
      jumpscare!
Headlights flash as these *fallacious* feelings roll
a train is barrelling towards,
I don't pick up my feet to run,
to these delusional thoughts of you
I succumb.
The train crashes into my emotions
I'll never know where I belong
              without *you*.

A sad skeleton

Crippling thoughts,
Heart gone shy
A fragile skeleton
Trudging over dirt mounts,
Slow, infirmary steps,
Scrawny bones amalgamated;
Paste of pure sorrow
Binded by tears.
Sticky mache mess
Not a care left,
Just another tumbleweed
Scraping seas of desert sand.
Me without you,
    I'm a human scribble
        Tangled in my flesh.

Cascade

Deary tears
   don't fret the
            f
               a
                 l
                 l

as his figure dwindles from mind
finally, you're released.
As once vigorous bones tire to brittle stone
my stiffening smile enfetters my soul,
tears, uncaged beasts,

               c
                 a
                     s
                       c
                      a
                    d
                     e

       my inner beavers are too weak.

Behind my bedroom door

Late glooming nights
urging thoughts splurge,
I scorn waking every morning,
imprints on paper
they scatter across my flooring;
sloppy ink trails
trembling hands

        scribbling,
            blistering,
                stinging

wanting more.
They kindle to feel again
what was once felt before.

Not dead yet

A hammock ties to both corners of my eyes.
They're bloodshot and strained,
desert sand skin
I'm exhausted.
I try staying vigilant
to protect these memories.
Shadow lions roar lullabies,
they will claw photographic thoughts
to shreds.
Rotten egg
penetrates my nasal follicles,
my hands become clammy uncontrollably.
The felines prey on these polaroid dreams;
a gallery with doors unhinged.
I pinch myself awake
before paw prints like the grim reaper
stride in.

Fractures in my chest

Agonising chest flutters
butterflies' hairline skeletons fossilise,
imprints of emptiness.
His name is guck in my throat
gulps **t h i c k** and ***sticky***,
ingesting this lust
I cough it up to clutch on.
the corpses crack and snap
never to forget him
with constant fractures in my chest.

Over-filled mugs & over-filled regrets

Old feelings arouse these temptations,
Feelings of familiarity.
Spiralling into a forbidden frenzy
The past kicks down my door.
I welcome it home humbly,
Pour it a mug of regret
Overflow the ceramic.
Seething water crisps my hands
    By accident.

I clench my eyelids
Potently grip to my clothes
Tear my favourite blonde jeans.
Incinerate this hankering!
Supremacy of stubbornness
We were born to be
Like mother and baby,
Please, cold past, cradle me.
    I ask politely.

Wind scolds my body
My windshield eyes become foggy.
Erase your pungent essence!
You narcotic, deceitful blessing

    Can we fall in love again
        from our first words said?

Binge eating

Saturated memories
Queasy when I bite,
Scrumptious and sickening.
Oily paper towel to scrub my eyes.
Memories contaminated but fragile,
I feast on my persuasion
I think I need you again,
The truth scours abrasions.
Sanitise my empty baking dish heart
I'm a belly full of guilt,
His delectable flavour
I've overeaten.

Forest green eyes stirred by Mother Earth

Crafty wooden hands carve another portrait.
Details of fine wrinkle lines
                            A tangible memory
Skin they no longer brush
Texture soft and plush.
Another sculpture for the gallery gathering,
An unforeseen congregation,
Blind sighted each signature signed.
My only photographs
And my aged memories
Mismatch the iris I painted on your sculpture,
The one colour I cannot mix right.
Sadness seeps through my splintered fingernails.
Murmuring in the sombre nights
                          I *will* be alright
Even my fraudulent art can't lift my arm,

Please
    Help me up,
                I *won't* be alright.

// Forest green eyes stirred by Mother Earth
        a colour I cannot replicate on this palette. //

Let me slip,
I'm not ready to get over it

Hide my quivery whispers,
I promise I'm not broken.
But with clothes ripped in half,
unshaved legs that won't outgrow the past,
I'm not convinced either.
I strap medical tape around my head.
This muffling mask over my mouth
will bandage up my heart
that still leaks my weeps in *italic*

I

    will

        survive.

How can I escape
when I'm bleeding your **final** words?
Bleach wafts and steam recrafts my hair,
others offer to mop me up.

    Please, leave me drenched,

        let me slip on my wretchedness.

Acknowledgments

I would like to thank my editor,
Rami H. Roushdi
for his invaluable input.

About the Author
Emily Bock

Growing up in North Queensland, Australia, Emily's whole life has been one long journey of understanding the world and practicing self-mastery. She's been writing fiction and poetry since a young age as a means of self expression and exploration, and has branched out into the fields of photography and calligraphy.

The limitlessness of creativity sets her free, just like the vastness of the world she is determined to experience.

Official Website:
*www.*hippiethinking.*com*

www.ingramcontent.com/pod-product-compliance
Lightning Source LLC
Chambersburg PA
CBHW010449010526
44118CB00019B/2522